HOW TO DRAW MONSTERS

HOW TO DRAW

DRACULA

Derrick Richards

Enslow PUBLISHING

Please visit our website, www.enslow.com. For a free color catalog of all our high-quality books, call toll free 1-800-398-2504 or fax 1-877-980-4454

Published in 2027 by
Enslow Publishing
2544 Clinton Street
Buffalo, NY 14224

Portions of this work were originally authored by Greg Roza and published as *Drawing Movie Monsters Step-by-Step: Drawing Dracula.* All new material in this edition is authored by Derrick Richards.

Cataloging-in-Publication Data
Names: Richards, Derrick.
Title: How to draw Dracula / Derrick Richards.
Description: Buffalo, NY : Enslow Publishing, 2027. | Series: How to draw monsters | Includes glossary and index.
Identifiers: ISBN 9781978548664 (pbk.) | ISBN 9781978548671 (library bound) | ISBN 9781978548688 (ebook)
Subjects: LCSH: Vampires in art--Juvenile literature. | Dracula, Count (Fictitious character)--Juvenile literature. | Monsters in art--Juvenile literature. | Drawing--Technique--Juvenile literature.
Classification: LCC NC825.V36 R534 2027 | DDC 743.87--dc23

Printed in China

Photo credits: Cover, p. 1 Stokkete/Shutterstock.com; cover, p. 1, 22 Shutterstock AI/Shutterstock.com; cover, p. 1, 5, 7, 9, 11, 13, 15, 17, 19, 21 (notebook) Liena10/Shutterstock.com; p. 5 (ruler) karen roach/Shutterstock.com; p. 5 (colored pencils) Avocado_studio/ Shutterstock.com; p. 5 (marker) New Africa/Shutterstock.com; p. 6 Wikipedia/Wikipedia; p. 8, 18 Shutterstock AI Generator/ Shutterstock.com; p. 10, 12, 14 Wikipedia/Wikipedia; p. 16 Michael Lynch/Shutterstock.com; p. 20 drawkman/Shutterstock.com

CPSIA compliance information: Batch #QSENS27: For further information, contact Enslow Publishing, New York, New York, at 1-800-398-2504.

Find us on

CONTENTS

Dracula the VAMPIRE

Vampires are scary mythical creatures. They have appeared in folktales and **legends** for hundreds of years. Many stories say that vampires are "undead," which means they are not fully alive or fully dead. These monsters sleep in **coffins** by day and can turn into bats in the night. In vampire stories, they use their **fangs** to bite their victims and then suck their blood!

The character Dracula first appeared in an 1897 book by Irish author Bram Stoker. Today, vampires are more popular than ever. Thanks to Stoker's book, people all over the world are fascinated by vampire stories. Let's learn to draw this classic movie monster in a few easy steps!

You will need the following supplies:

PAPER

PENCIL

RULER

MARKER

COLORED PENCILS

THE FIRST DRACULA

Bram Stoker's *Dracula* was the novel that started it all. It **inspired** many more vampire books and movies throughout the years. There were even plays based on the book.

In 1927, Hungarian actor Bela Lugosi starred as Count Dracula in a Broadway play. He did such a good job that he drew the attention of filmmakers who wanted to make a movie about Dracula. He was asked to star in the 1931 movie *Dracula*. His performance in the movie made him a monster-movie legend.

Let's start by drawing Bela Lugosi as he strikes a classic Dracula pose.

One of the first horror movies ever made was a vampire movie called *Nosferatu* (noss-fuh-RAH-too). In 1922, people thought this German film was very scary!

Step 1

Draw the outline of the head. Add a rounded shape for the body.

Step 2

Add small circles and ovals around the body.

Step 3

Join the circles to form the arms and legs. Add the outlines of the hands and shoes. Draw the outline of the cape.

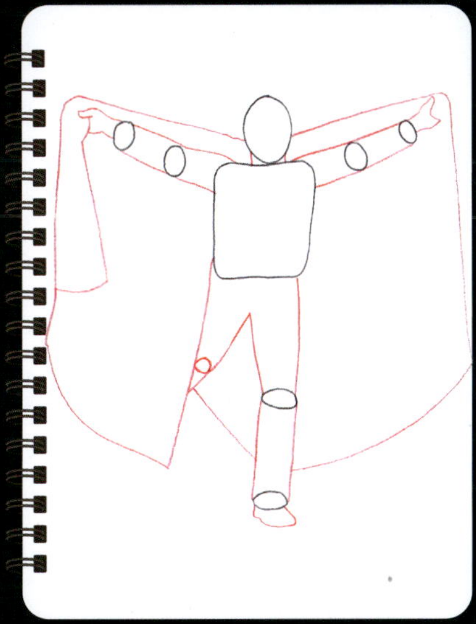

Step 4

Draw the hairline, the collar of the cape, and the vest. Add details to the coat and the cape.

Step 5

Draw the eyes, nose, and mouth. Add details to the clothes. Erase the guides.

Step 6

Add details to the facial features. Draw the folds in the clothing.

THE VAMPIRE'S COFFIN

In the 1931 movie *Dracula*, a man named Renfield stays at Castle Dracula in Eastern Europe. Vampires are said to be able to control the people they bite, and in this movie, Renfield is being controlled by Dracula. Dracula and Renfield later travel to England by ship. Dracula hides in a coffin and feeds on sailors' blood at night.

In many stories about Dracula, the vampire sleeps in a coffin during the day to keep away from the sunlight. Let's try drawing Dracula as he rises from his coffin at nighttime.

Vampires aren't always scary—sometimes they can be portrayed as funny or silly, too!

Step 1

Draw shapes as shown to begin the head and body.

Step 2

Draw small ovals around the body to act as guides.

Step 3

Join the ovals to form arms and part of Dracula's leg. Draw hands. Draw two lines for the neck.

Step 4

Draw the coffin. Add the hairline and jacket.

Step 5

Draw the facial features. Add details to the hands, clothes, and coffin. Erase guide ovals.

Step 6

Add details to Dracula's face and the coffin. Add color.

A MONSTER SUCCESS

Most people who saw *Dracula* thought Bela Lugosi played a very scary vampire. In the movie, Lugosi spoke slowly and with his own Hungarian **accent**. This helped make his performance even more believable to the audience.

When many people think about vampires, they often picture the type of vampire that Lugosi created for his role in *Dracula*. His performance became the basis for how we think of vampires today, nearly 100 years later!

Now, let's draw the vampire as he walks out of his coffin.

Lugosi was from the Eastern European country of Hungary. Hungary is near Transylvania, which is where Dracula was from in the story.

Step 1

Draw a round shape for the head and a boxy shape for the body.

Step 2

Draw small circles and ovals around the body.

Step 3

Use the circles and ovals to guide you in drawing the arms, legs, hands, and feet. Add the neck and cape.

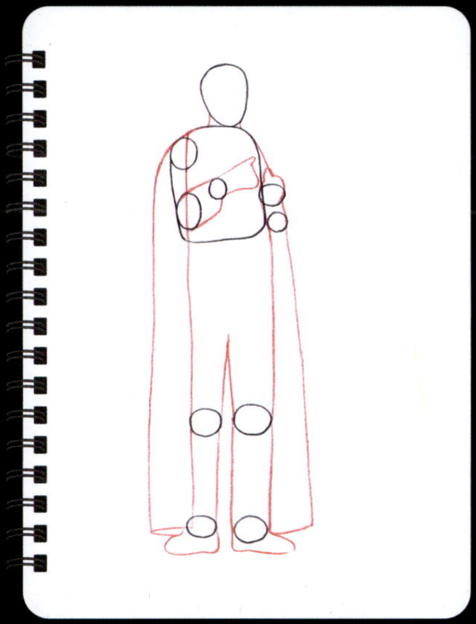

Step 4

Draw the hair. Add fingers to the hands. Add the cape's collar and the outline of the vest. Draw the outline of the coffin.

Step 5

Draw eyes, eyebrows, the nose, and the mouth. Add details to the clothes and the coffin. Erase the guide shapes.

Step 6

Add the fangs and other facial features. Add more details to the clothing and coffin.

THE FAMOUS MONSTER

Dracula turned Bela Lugosi into a huge horror movie star. He appeared in a total of 18 movies. Besides Dracula, he played many other scary movie characters, including Frankenstein. But he is most famous for his vampire roles.

In 1944, Lugosi played a vampire in the movie *The Return of the Vampire*. In 1948, Lugosi played Dracula again in a comedy called *Abbott and Costello Meet Frankenstein*. He played a vampire in movies four times, twice as the famous Count Dracula.

Now, let's draw Bela Lugosi in his most famous role.

Dracula helped other movie monsters become popular, too. These include the Mummy and the Wolf Man. Fans love to be scared!

Step 1

Draw the head, and begin to draw the body.

Step 2

Draw round shapes as shown. These will help you draw the arms and legs.

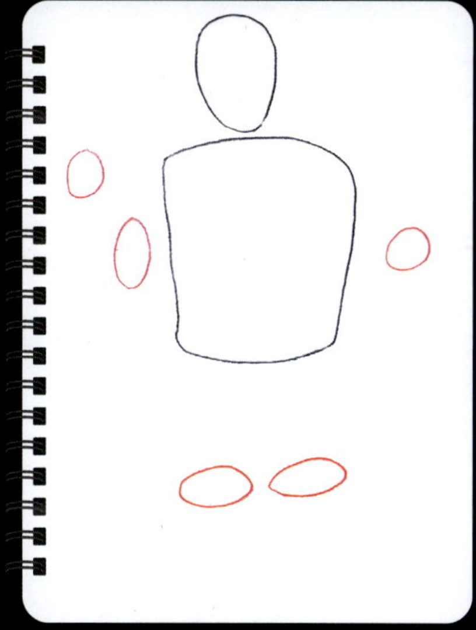

Step 3

Join the round shapes to form arms and legs. Add lines for the neck.

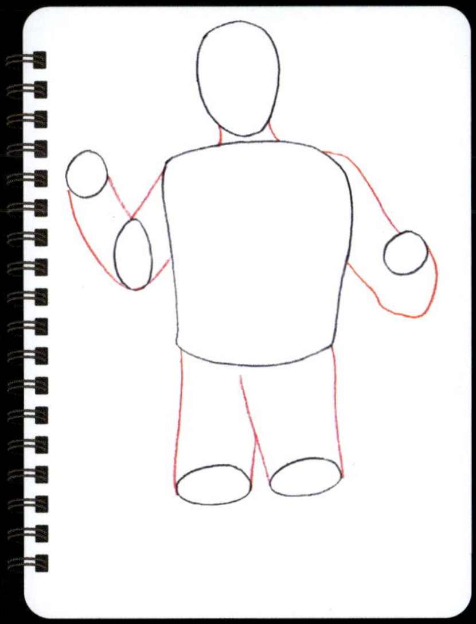

Step 4

Draw the hairline and the outline of the face. Add hands. Draw the outlines of the bowtie, jacket, and cape.

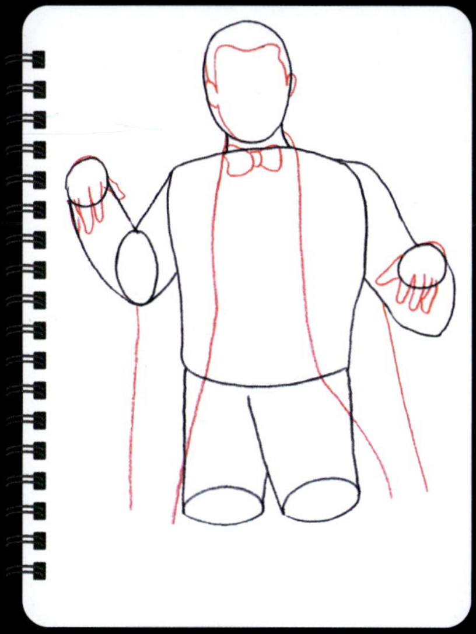

Step 5

Add the eyes, eyebrows, nose, and mouth. Give Dracula long fingernails. Draw the vest. Add the collar and other details to the coat. Erase the guides.

Step 6

Add the final details to the face and the clothes. Color your drawing.

THE LEGEND CONTINUES

In the 1950s, British filmmakers began making new **versions** of the classic movie monster. A whole new era of vampires began!

In 1958, British actor Christopher Lee starred as the famous vampire in the movie *Dracula*. It was called *The Horror of Dracula* in the United States so that it wouldn't be confused with the 1931 movie *Dracula*. This British Dracula movie was an instant hit all over the world!

Dracula didn't always have to bite people. Sometimes he put spells on people so that he could control them. Let's draw Dracula as he puts a spell on his victim.

Thanks to the success of *The Horror of Dracula*, Christopher Lee appeared in several more Dracula movies. He also appeared in more **modern** movies such as *Star Wars* and *Lord of the Rings*.

Step 1

Draw an oval for the head. Add a shape for the outline of the body.

Step 2

Draw circles and ovals around the body.

Step 3

Join the circles and ovals to form the arms, legs, hands, and feet. Draw the outline of the cape and the vest.

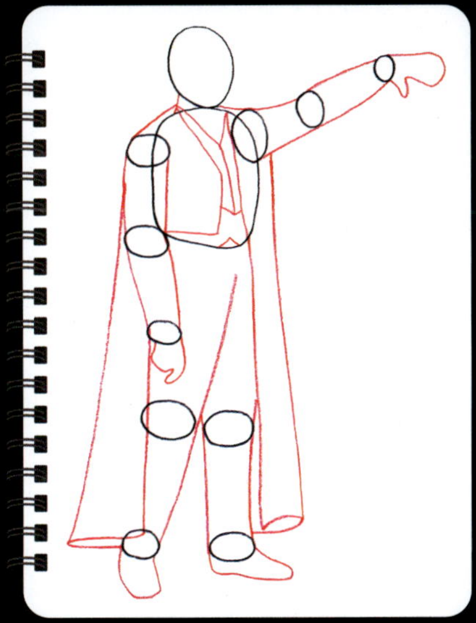

Step 4

Add the fingers. Draw the outline of Dracula's face and hair. Draw the collar of the cape.

Step 5

Draw the eyes, nose, and mouth. Add detail to the clothing. Erase extra lines.

Step 6

Add more details to Dracula's face and clothes.

VAMPIRE BATS

In stories and movies, it's said that Dracula can turn into a bat and fly. The vampire bat is a real-life animal that is named after the famous monster. Like Dracula, vampire bats feed on blood!

Unfortunately, their names give vampire bats a bad **reputation**. These creatures aren't as scary as they sound. Vampire bats rarely bite humans, and they only eat about a spoonful of blood at a time. Also, vampire bats don't suck blood like their **namesakes** do. Instead, they lap it up like a cat!

Let's try drawing one of these flying **mammals**.

There are three species of vampire bat: the hairy-legged vampire bat, the white-winged vampire bat, and the common vampire bat. They all feed on blood!

Step 1

Begin your drawing with two round shapes.

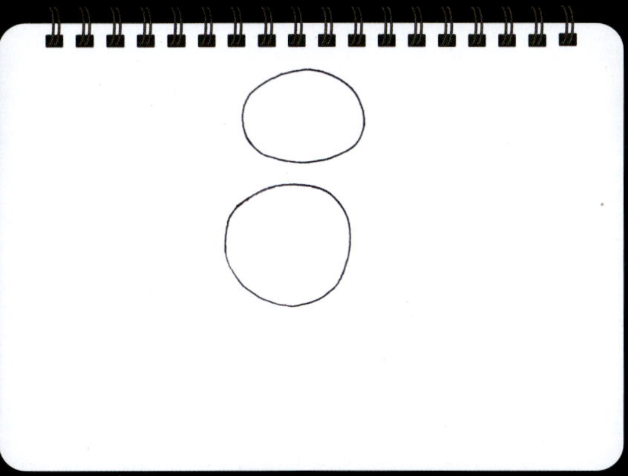

Step 2

Draw lines as shown to form the outline of the bat's wings.

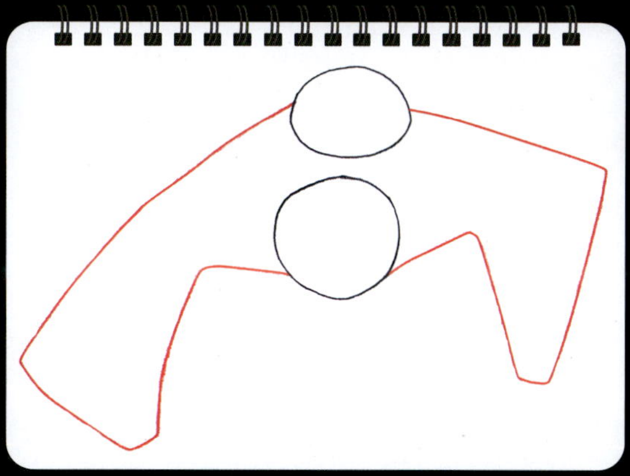

Step 3

Draw the folds in the bat's wings. Add the outline of the feet.

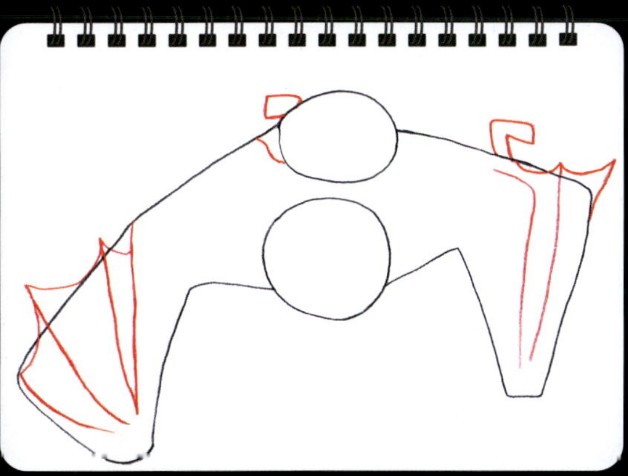

Step 4

Draw the outline of the bat's face in the lower circle. Erase extra lines.

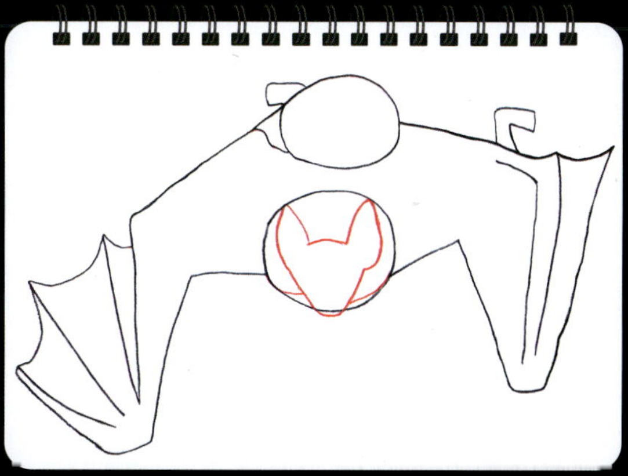

Step 5

Draw the bat's ears, eyes, nose, mouth, and feet. Add folds to the wings. Erase extra lines.

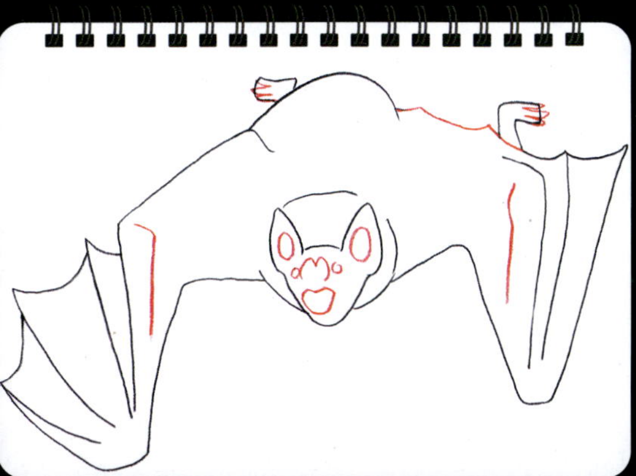

Step 6

Add details to the facial features and wings. Give the bat fangs, and add fur to its body.

ONE OF THE BEST

In 1992, British actor Gary Oldman brought a new look to the part of Dracula. His version of Dracula in the movie *Bram Stoker's Dracula* looked scarier than ever before. Some fans think it is the best vampire movie ever made. It even won three Academy Awards!

The 1992 movie is a lot like Bram Stoker's original book in many ways. For example, Dracula grows younger during the course of the movie, just as he does in Stoker's book. But the movie has its differences, too.

Dracula needs sharp fangs to bite his victims. Let's draw Dracula on the hunt.

Dracula didn't always have long, scary fangs. In the 1931 movie, Dracula didn't have fangs at all! Long, sharp fangs emerged in movies in the 1950s to make vampires look even scarier.

Step 1

Draw an egg shape for the head.

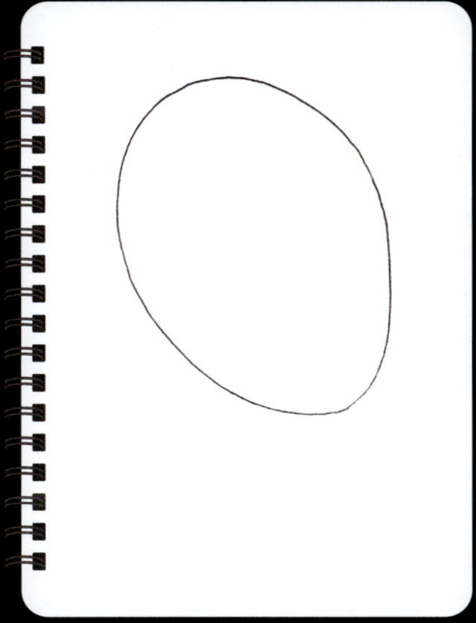

Step 2

Add shapes to begin the ear, eyes, and mouth.

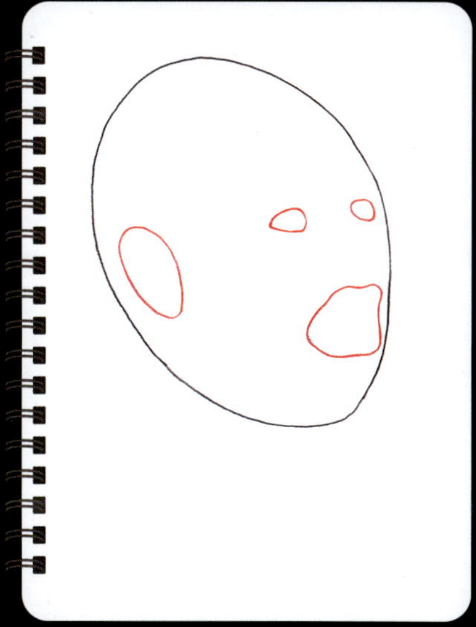

Step 3

Add the hair, eyebrows, nose, and neck. Draw the outline of the cape's collar.

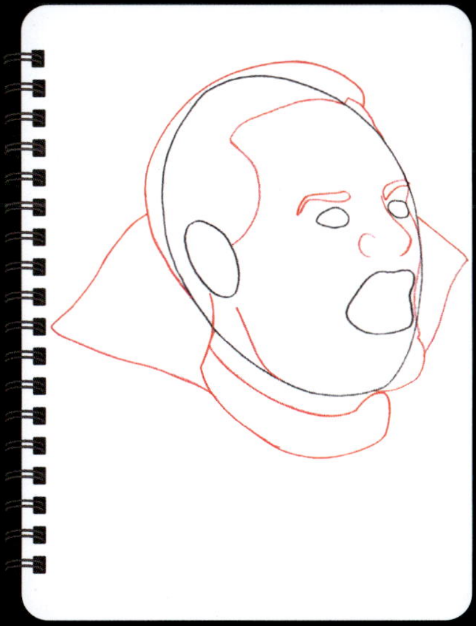

Step 4

Draw Dracula's bowtie. Add lines to his ears and around his mouth.

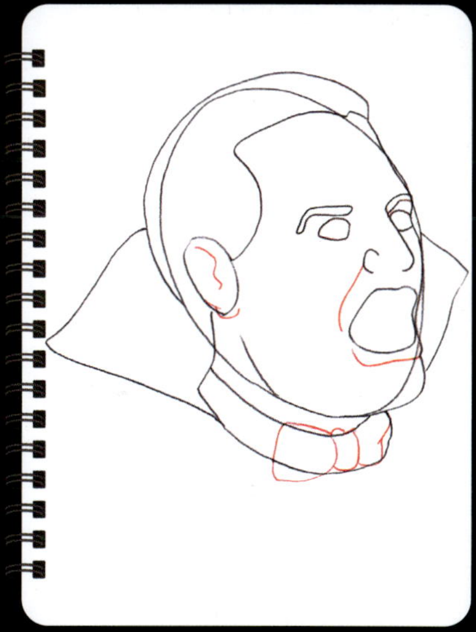

Step 5

Add to the eyes, nose, mouth, ears, and neck as shown. Erase extra lines.

Step 6

Give Dracula sharp fangs. Add the final details to his face and clothes. Color your drawing.

DRACULA LIVES ON

Bram Stoker's 1897 novel led to Dracula as a cultural **icon**. Since then, hundreds of vampire movies have been made. More than 100 years later, these creatures continue to appear in modern books and movies such as *Twilight* and *Hotel Transylvania*. People continue to be fascinated with these fearsome monsters of the night.

But Dracula isn't just a famous movie star. His likeness can be found on TV, in cartoons and comics, and in video games. Dracula has even inspired a breakfast cereal called Count Chocula, which can be found in stores during the Halloween season. The "undead" vampire continues to live on!

Now, let's draw Dracula in his final moments.

Dracula has appeared in more than 200 movies. That's more than any other movie monster!

Step 1

Draw the outline of the head and body.

Step 2

Connect the head to the body with two lines. Add guide shapes as shown.

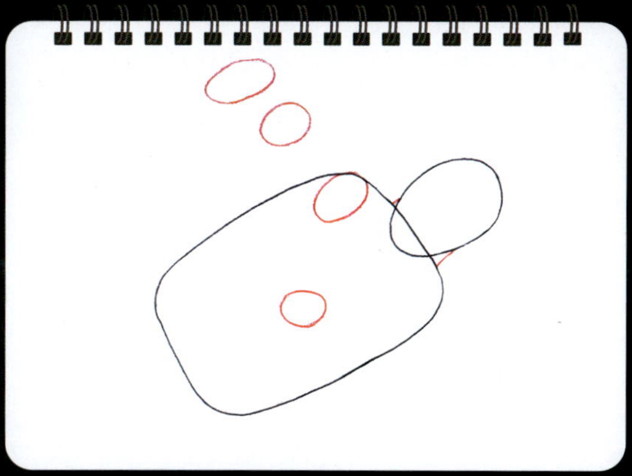

Step 3

Using the guide shapes, draw Dracula's arms and hands. Draw the coffin.

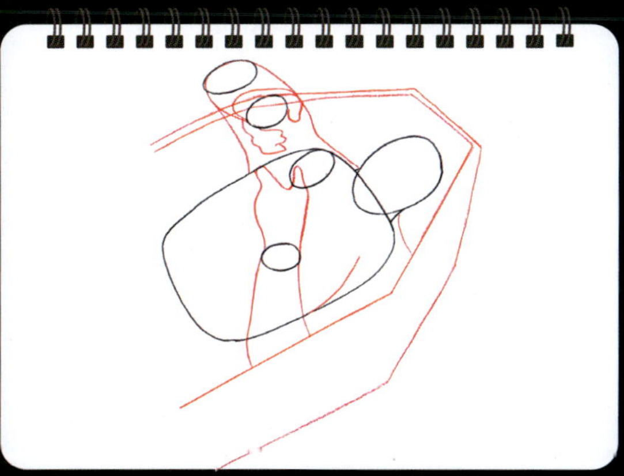

Step 4

Add the hair and ears. Draw fingers. Draw the clothes.

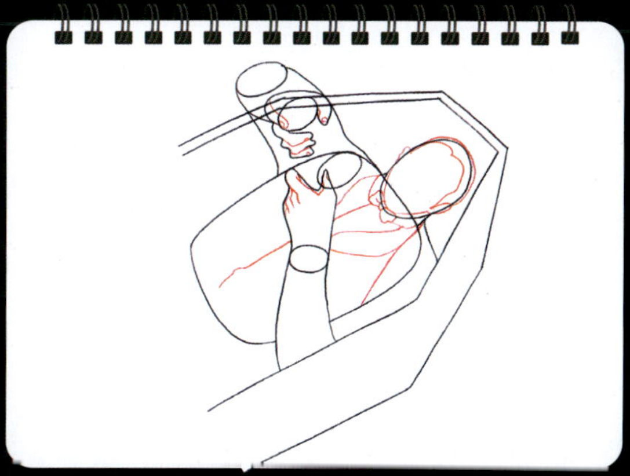

Step 5

Draw the stake in Dracula's hands. Draw the face, and give Dracula fangs. Add lines to the clothes and coffin. Erase the guides and any other extra lines.

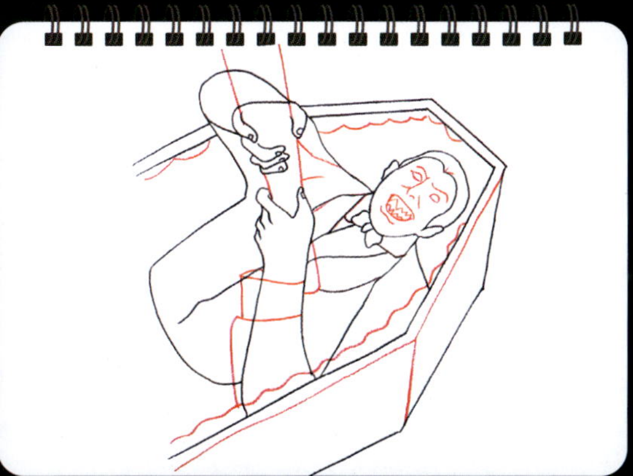

Step 6

Add finishing details to the face, hands, clothes, and coffin.

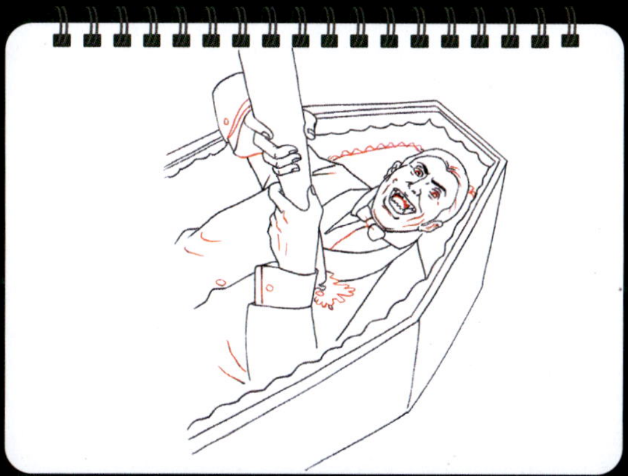

DID YOU KNOW?

The name "Dracula" means "dragon" or "devil" in Romanian.

Bela Lugosi almost never blinks during his performance in the 1931 movie *Dracula*. He did this to appear scarier.

The name of Count Dracula was inspired by a real person. Vlad III Dracula was a prince in Eastern Europe during the mid-1400s who was known as "Vlad the **Impaler.**"

In some stories, Dracula is allergic to garlic!

GLOSSARY

accent (AK-sent) A way of speaking that reflects where a person is from.

coffin (KAH-fun) A box that holds a dead body.

fangs (FANGZ) Sharp, hollow, or grooved teeth that inject venom.

horror (HOHR-ur) A strong feeling of shock or fear.

icon (EYE-kahn) Something that is widely admired for having influence.

impaler (im-PAY-lur) One who has impaled another person. To impale means to drive a sharp object through something.

inspired (in-SPY-erd) To have moved someone to do something.

legend (LEH-jend) A story, passed down through the years, that cannot be proved.

mammal (MAM-uhl) A warm-blooded animal that has hair or fur and usually gives birth to live babies.

modern (MAH-durn) New, or having to do with the recent times.

namesake (NAME-sayk) A person or thing that has the same name as another.

reputation (rep-yuh-TAY-shuhn) Your worth or character as judged by other people.

version (VER-zhun) A thing that is different from something else, or has different forms.

INDEX

ON THE INTERNET

Dracula (Short Kids Version)

https://ririro.com/kids-books/dracula/

Read a short, kid-friendly version of Bram Stoker's *Dracula.*

Dracula Facts for Kids

https://kids.kiddle.co/Dracula

Learn more about the history of Dracula and see a list of some of the most well-known Dracula movies.

Publisher's note to educators and parents: Our editors have carefully reviewed these websites to ensure that they are suitable for students. Many websites change frequently, however, and we cannot guarantee that a site's future contents will continue to meet our high standards of quality and educational value. Be advised that students should be closely supervised whenever they access the internet.